YOU ARE AN ARTIST

BY
YINKA ILORI

TATE

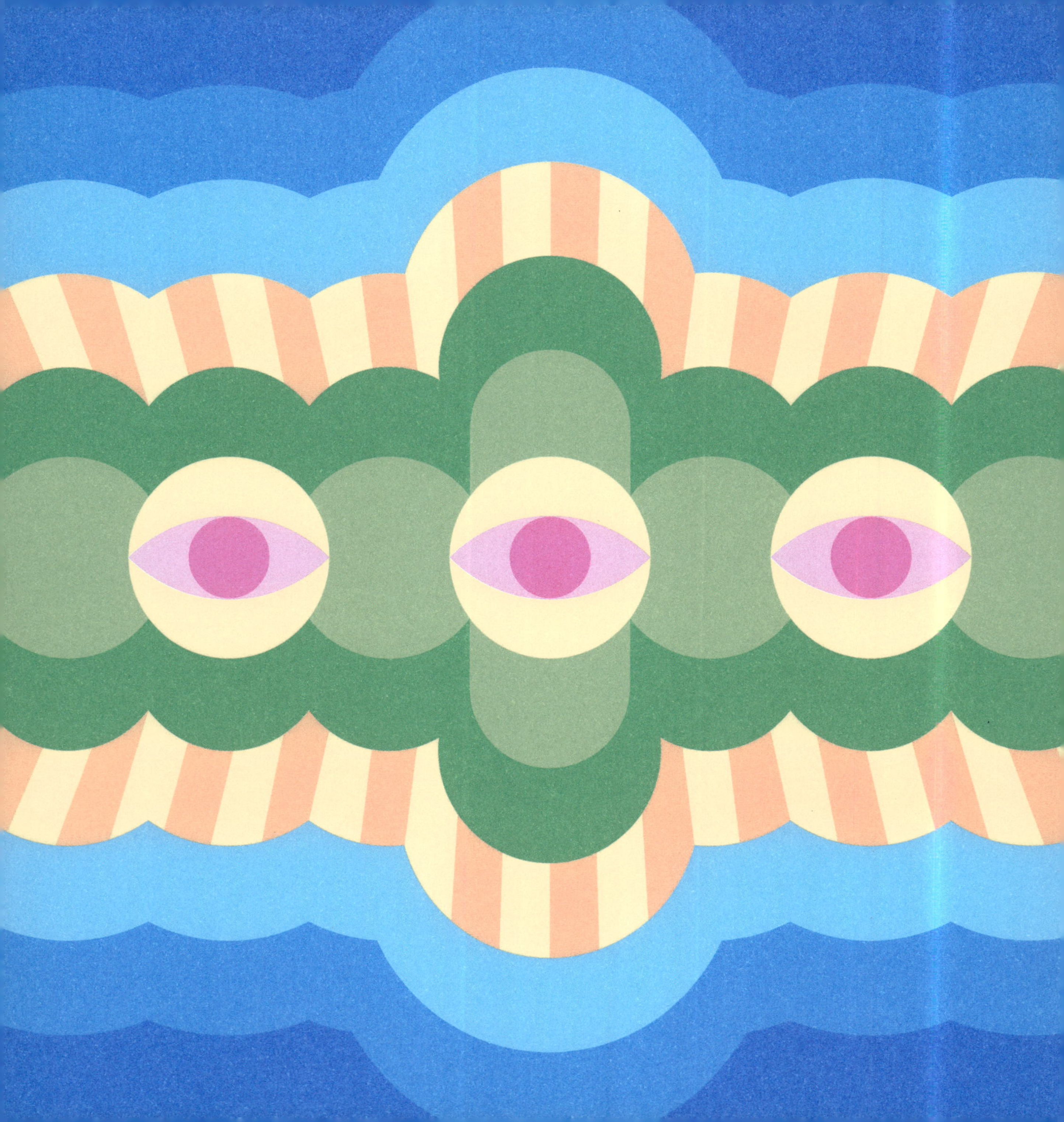

YOUR DREAMS CAN SEE YOU,
SO KEEP DREAMING.

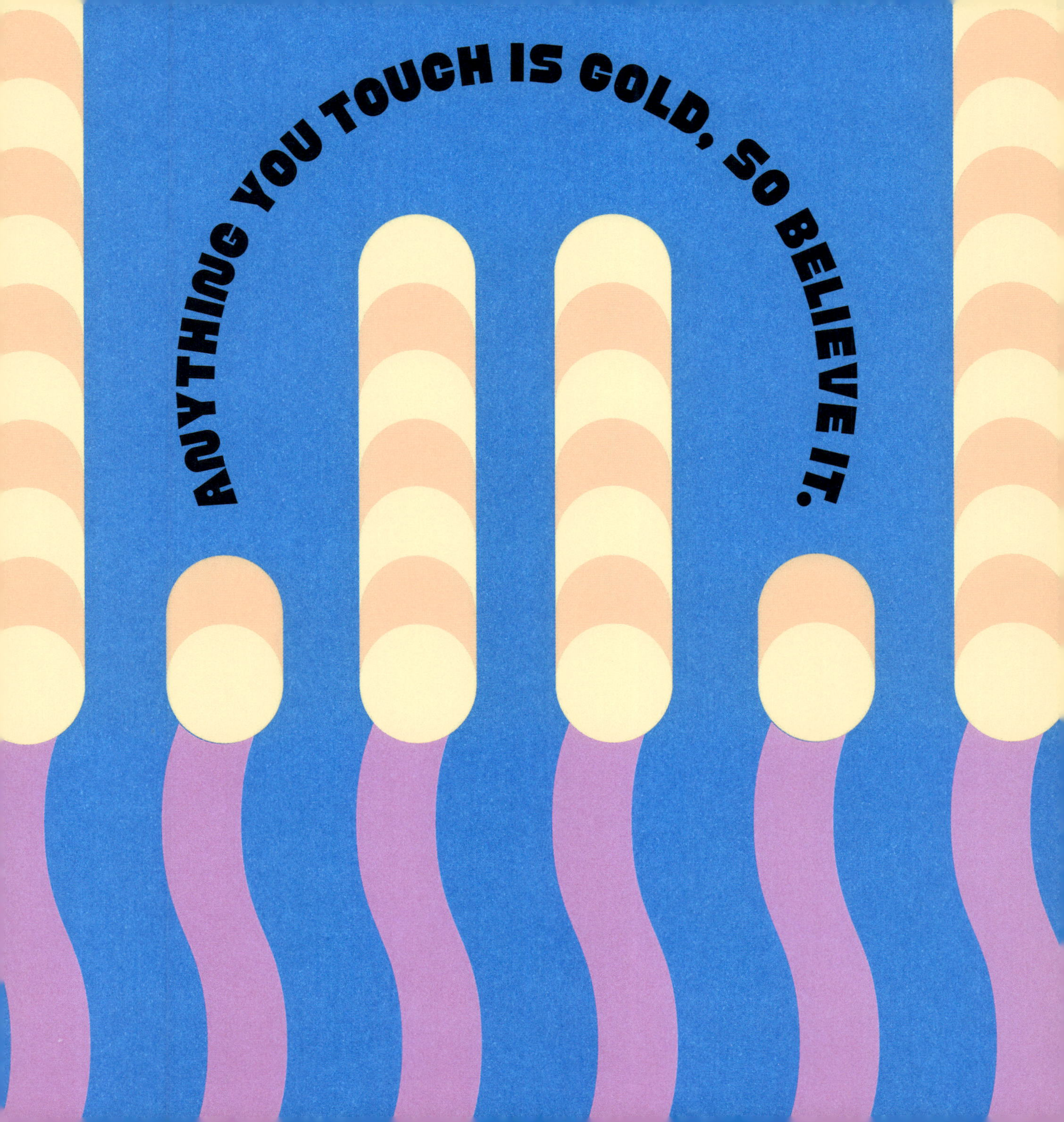
ANYTHING YOU TOUCH IS GOLD, SO BELIEVE IT.

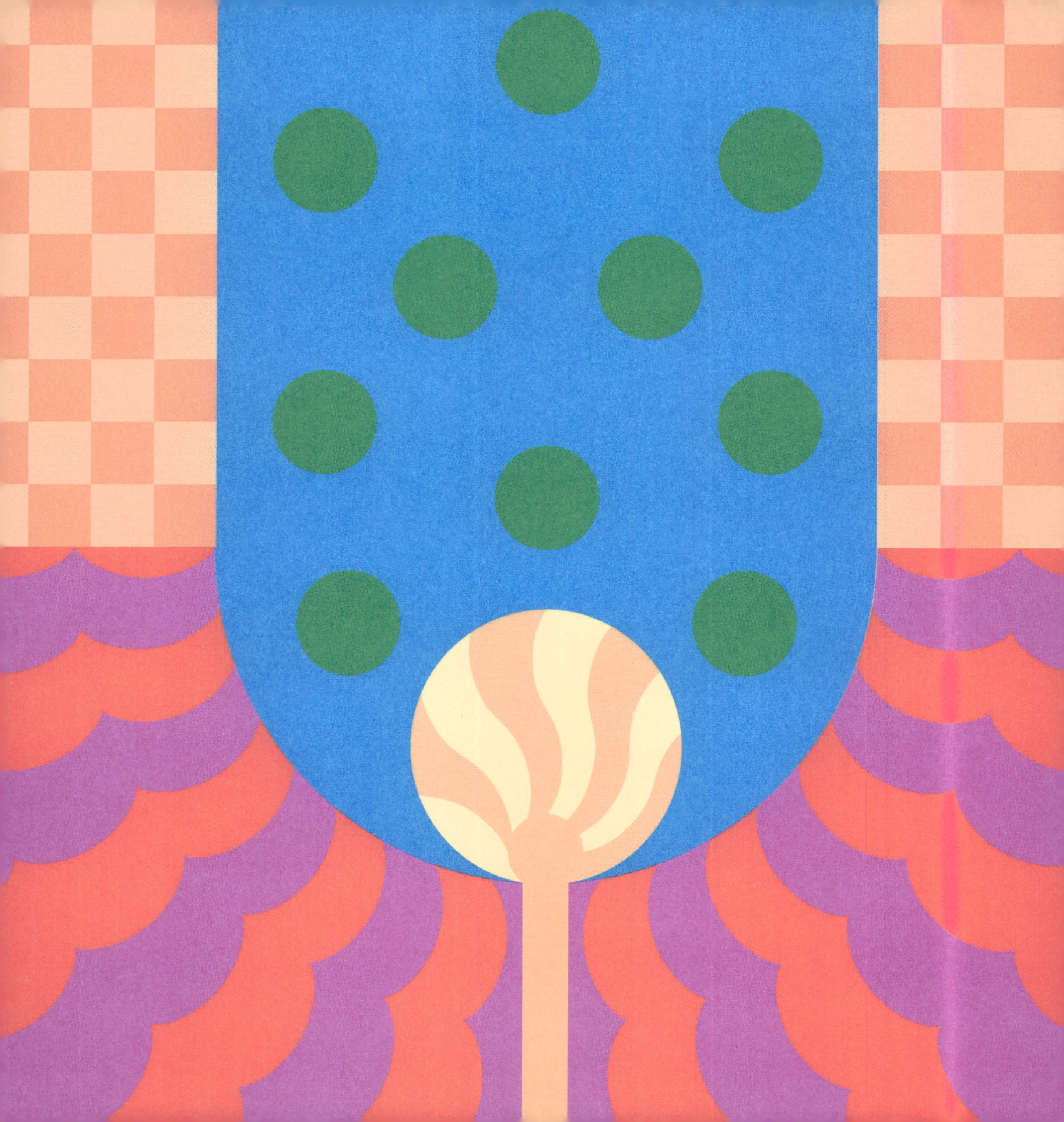

YOU ARE MAGIC.
KEEP SHINING YOUR LIGHT.
REST IS NEEDED FOR CREATIVITY.
IT'S OKAY TO SLOW DOWN
AND TAKE A BREAK.

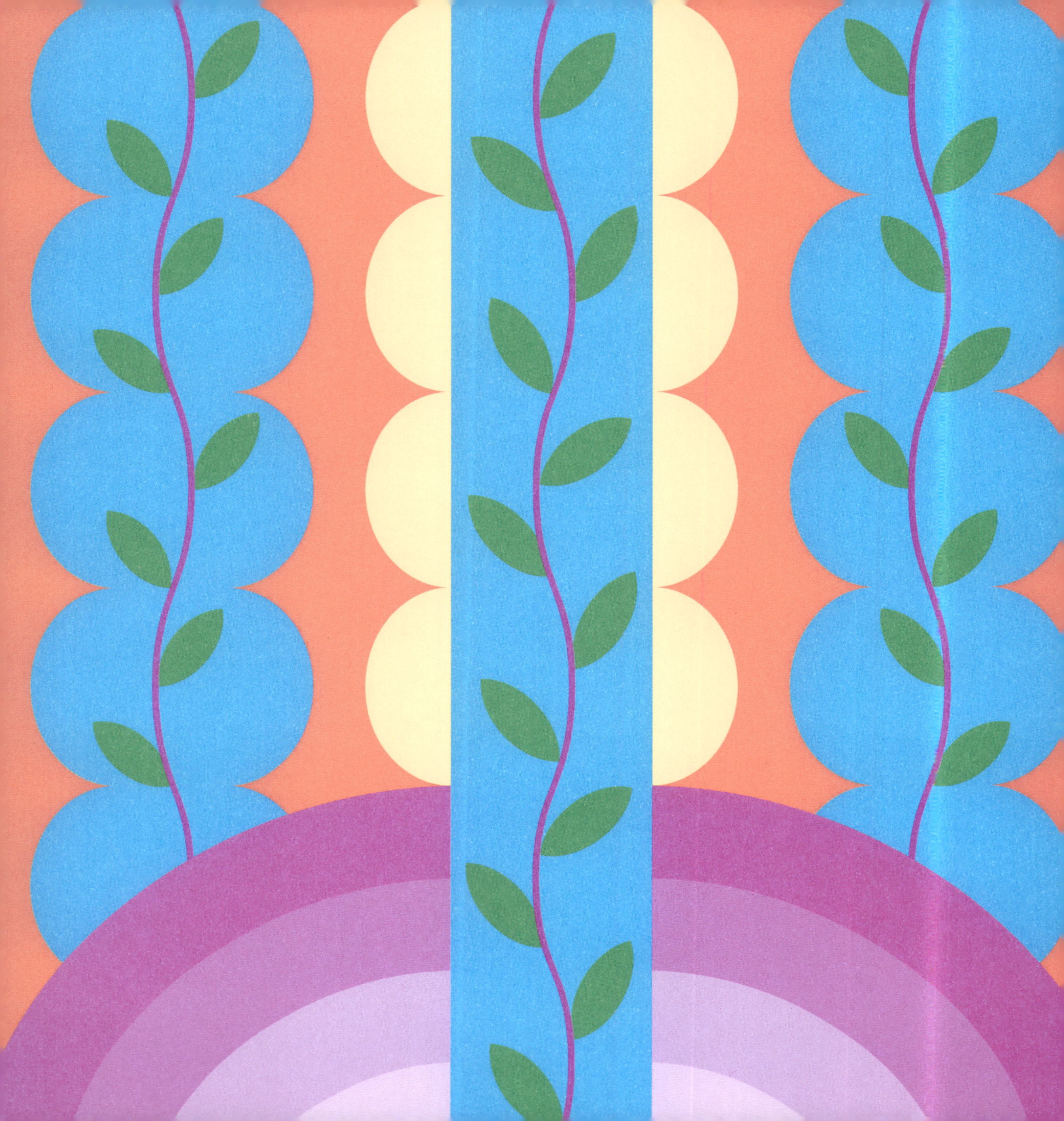

PRAISE YOURSELF. IT'S OKAY TO DO SO.

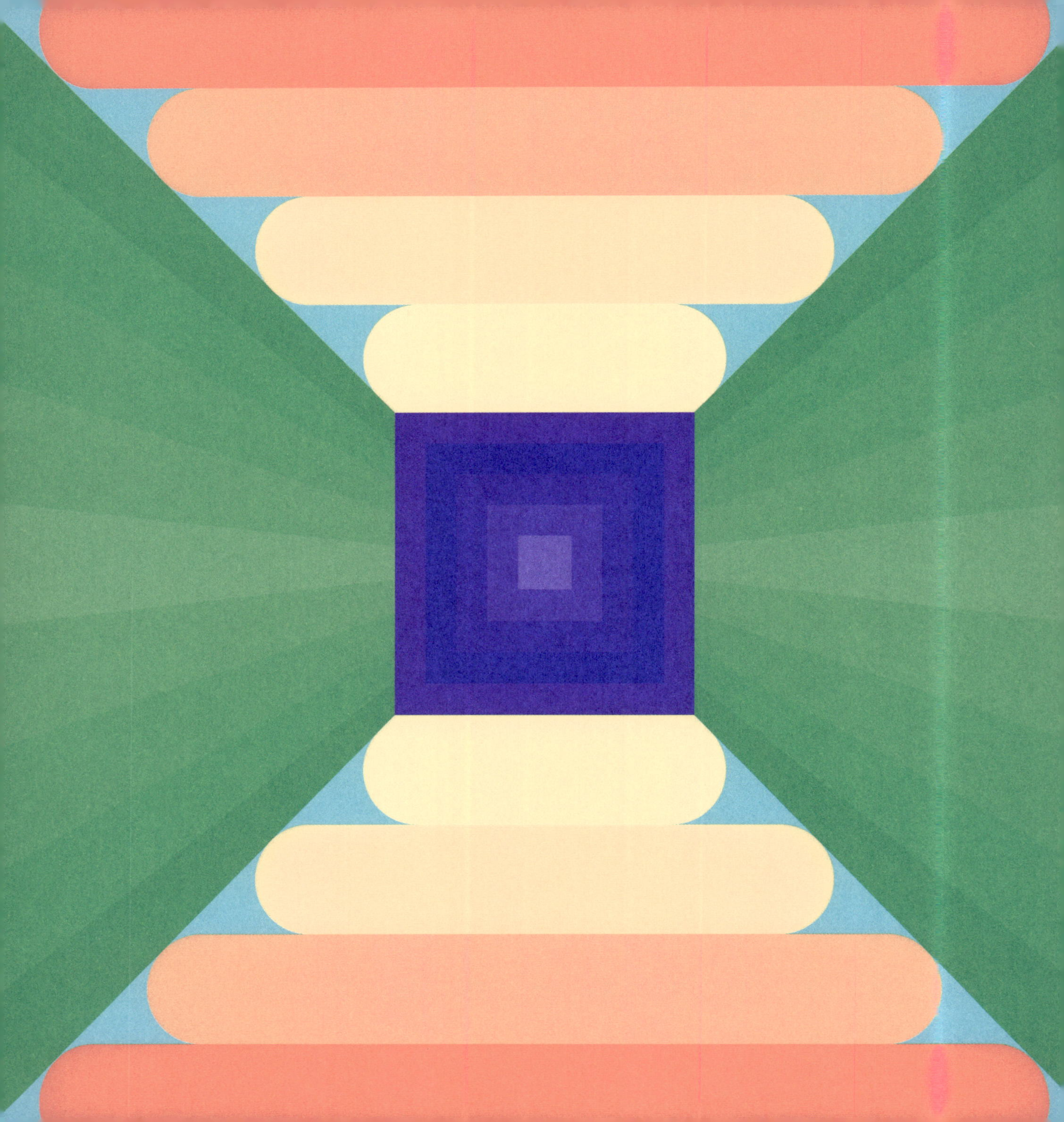

YOU DESERVE TO
BE HERE.
WALK WITH YOUR
HEAD HELD HIGH.

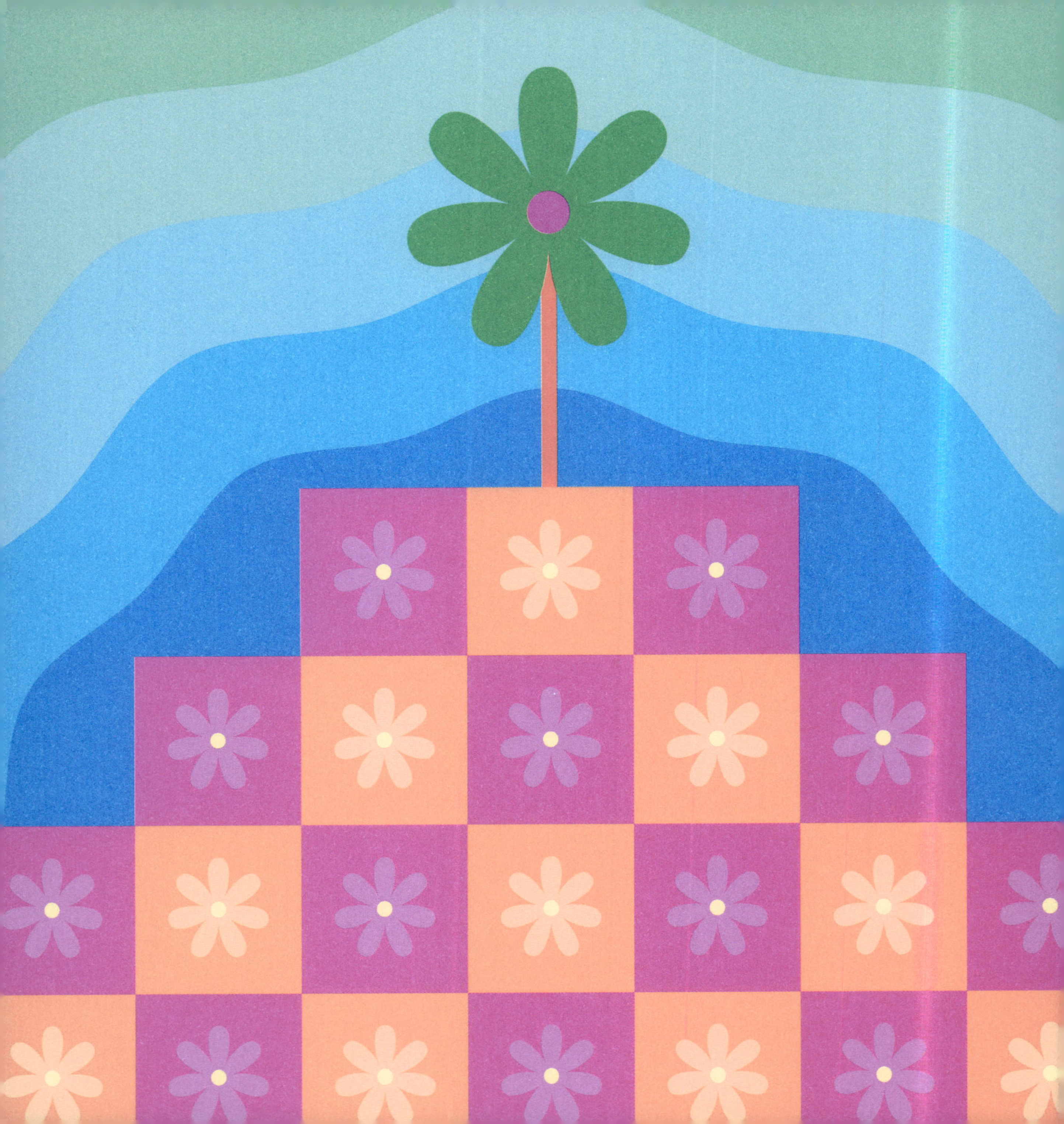

GROW YOUR FLOWERS

AND TRUST IN YOURSELF.

THERE IS ONLY ONE YOU.

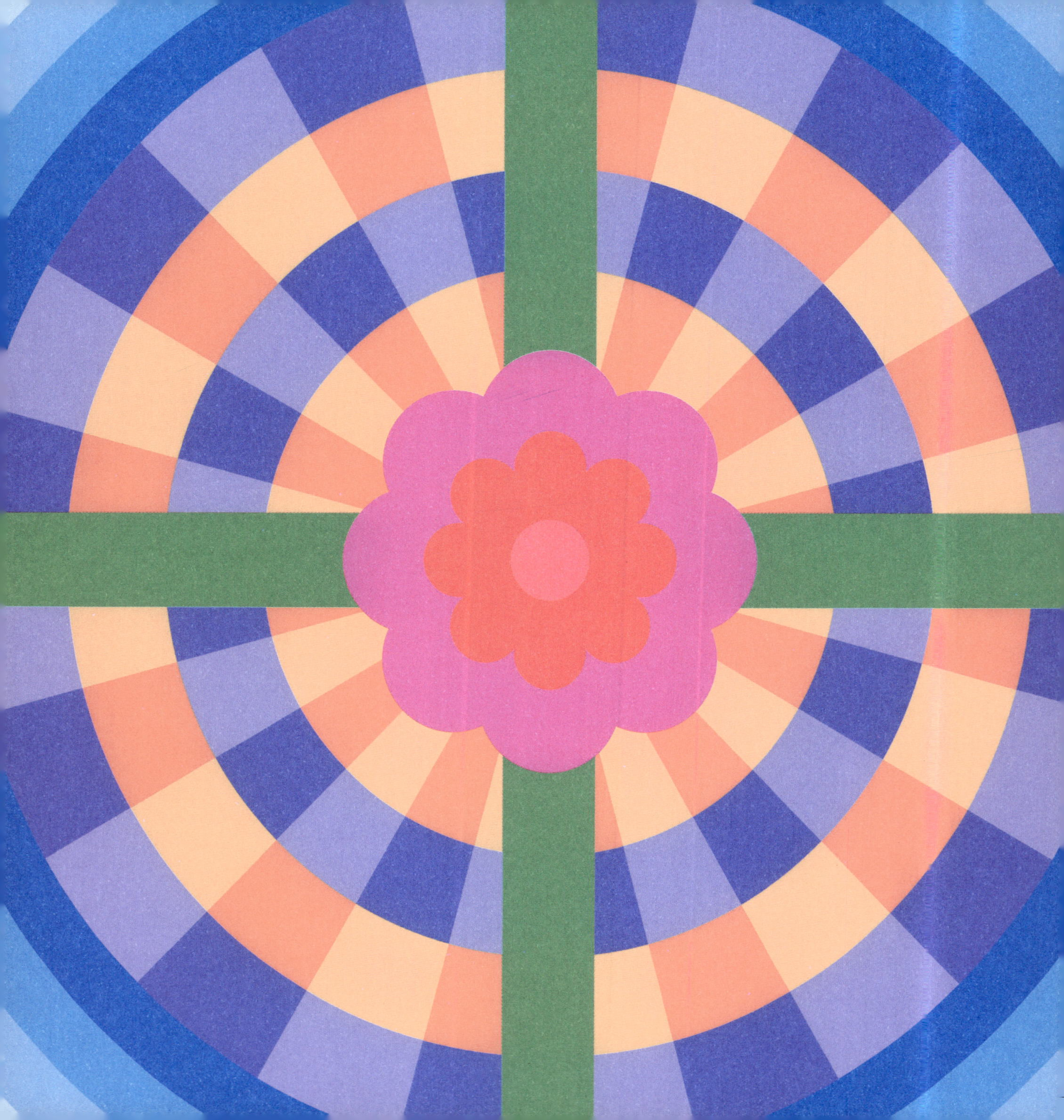

WE CAN ALL SEE THE GREATNESS IN YOU AND YOUR ART SO KEEP PUSHING ON.

WINNING DOESN'T ALWAYS MEAN SUCCESS. SUCCESS CAN BE COUNTED AS THE FULFILMENT ART BRINGS TO YOUR LIFE.

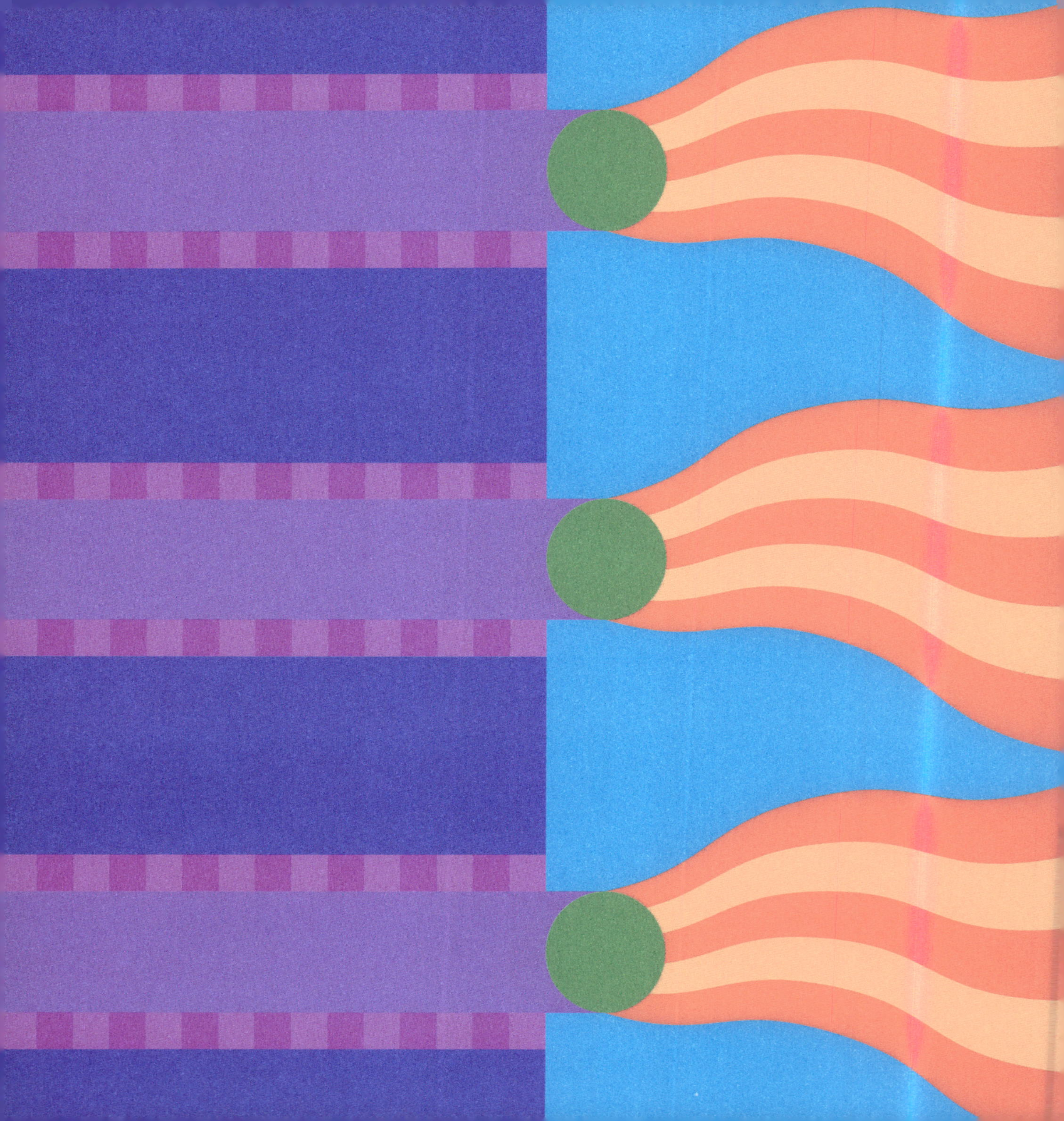

THE PATH YOU TAKE TODAY DOES NOT DEFINE WHO YOU ARE TOMORROW. SO, TAKE YOUR TIME AND CHERISH YOUR OWN ARTISTIC JOURNEY.

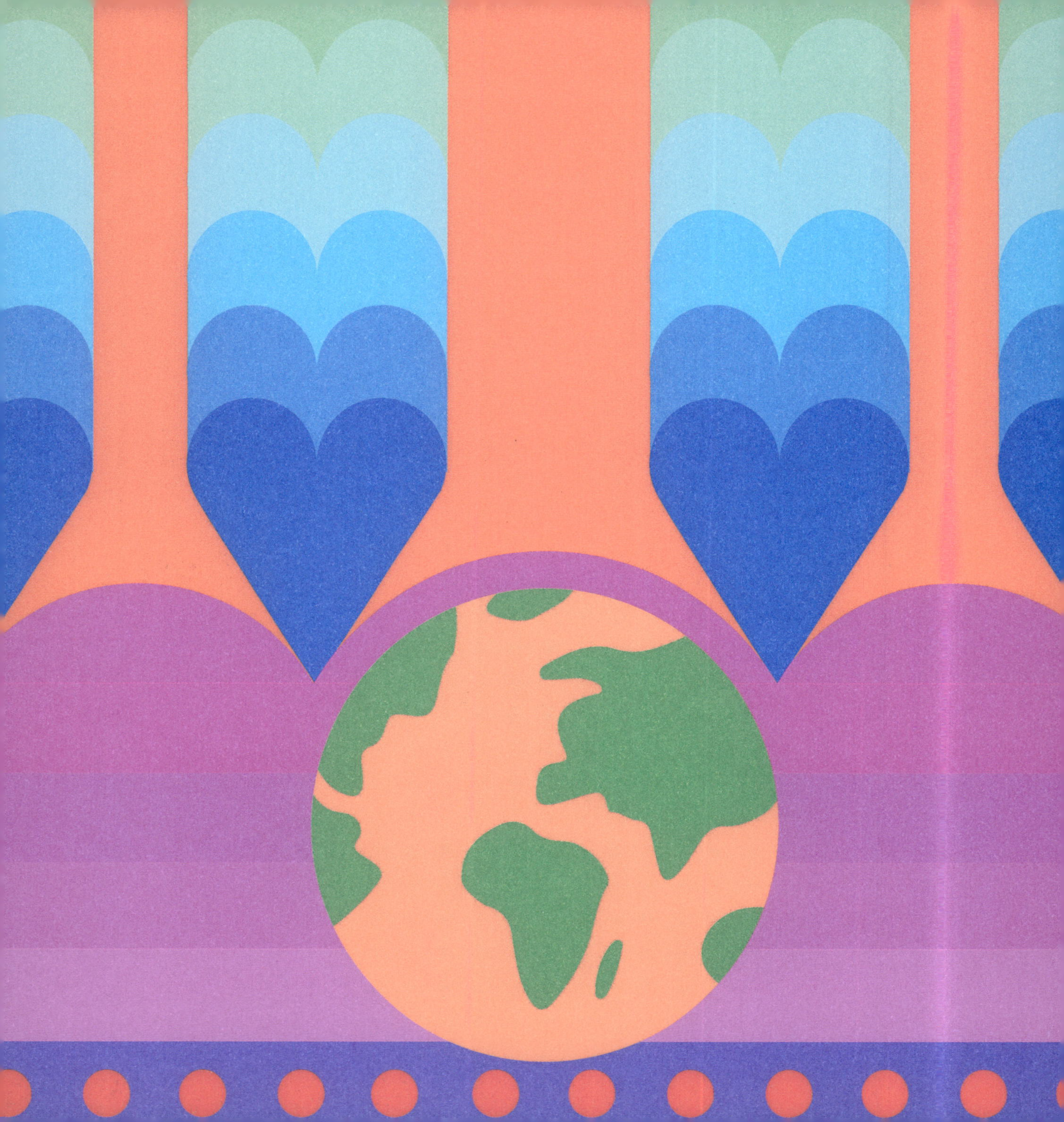

BEING YOU IS ENOUGH FOR THE WORLD. YOUR ART IS A GIFT, SO HOLD IT TIGHTLY WITH BOTH HANDS.

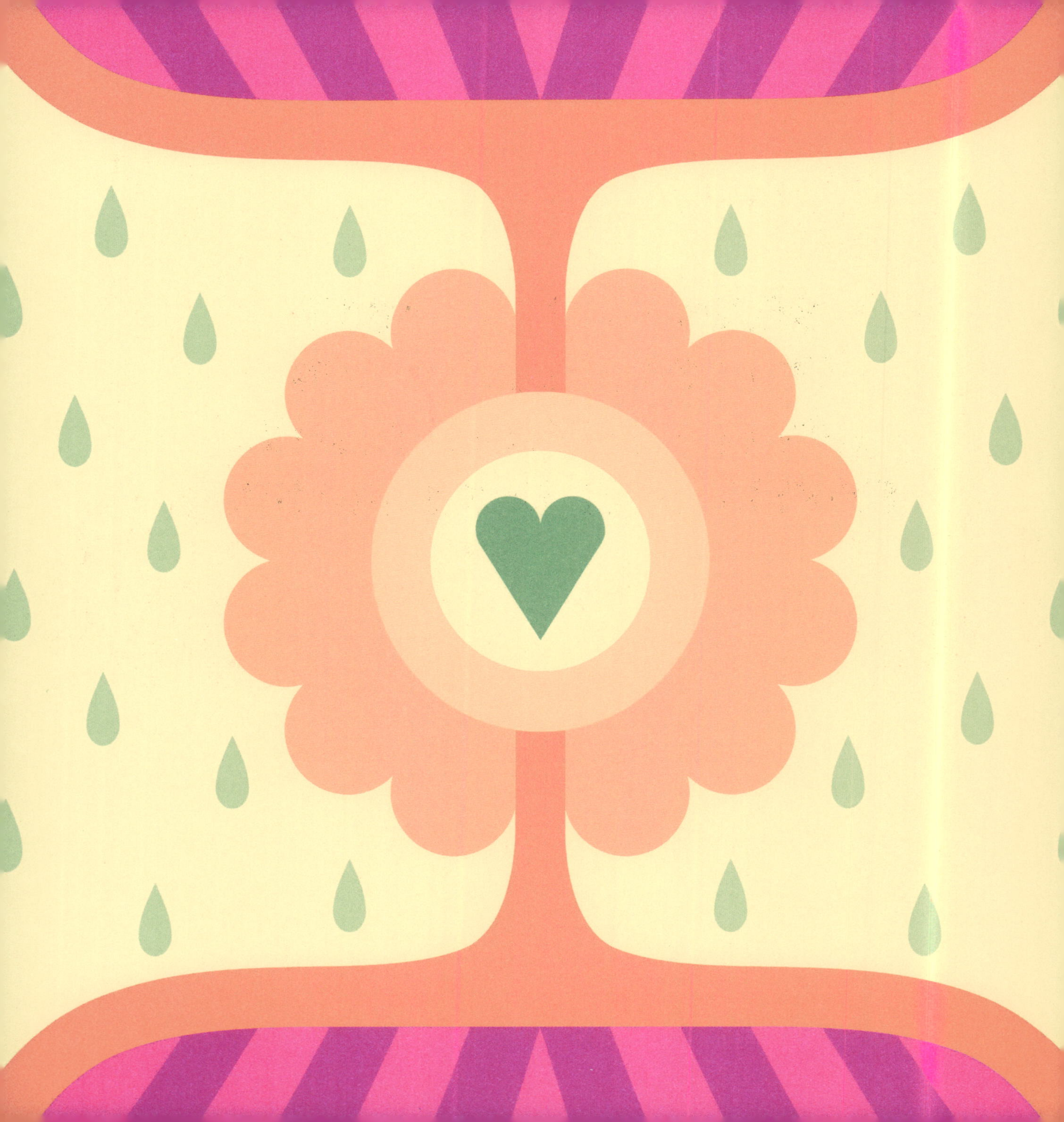

DON'T LET
OTHERS DEFINE YOU.
YOU ARE AN ARTIST
AND ART IS
FOR EVERYONE.

First published 2025 by order of the Tate Trustees by Tate Publishing, a division of Tate Enterprises Ltd, Millbank, London SW1P 4RG

www.tate.org.uk

Production: Juliette Dupire
Editors: Emilia Will and Cherise Lopes Baker
Assistant Editor: Aki Gurung

A catalogue record for this book is available from the British Library

ISBN 978 1 84976 912 9

Distributed in the United States and Canada by ABRAMS, New York
Library of Congress Control Number applied for

Colour reproduction by Evergreen Colour Management Ltd
Printed and bound in China by C&C Offset Printing Co., Ltd

FSC www.fsc.org MIX Paper | Supporting responsible forestry FSC® C008047

THIS BOOK IS DEDICATED TO MY BELOVED MOTHER - THE FIRST WOMAN TO LOVE ME AND THE REASON WHY I DREAM SO BIG. THANK YOU FOR TEACHING AND SHOWING ME THE POWER OF DREAMING.

LOVE YOU,
YOUR SON